HOW OUR BODIES WORK

FOOD and DIGESTION

JAN BURGESS

Editorial planning
Philip Steele

M
MACMILLAN

First published 1989
Reprinted 1989

Published by
MACMILLAN EDUCATION LTD
Houndmills, Basingstoke, Hampshire RG21 2XS
and London
Companies and representatives
throughout the world

Designed and produced by BLA Publishing Limited,
East Grinstead, Sussex, England.

Also in LONDON · HONG KONG · TAIPEI · SINGAPORE · NEW YORK

A Ling Kee Company

Illustrations by Sebastian Quigley/Linden Artists; Sallie Alane Reason and Linda Thursby/Linden Artists
Printed in Hong Kong

British Library Cataloguing in Publication Data

Burgess, Jan
    Food and digestion. — (How our bodies
    work). — (Macmillan world library)
    1. Digestive organs — Juvenile literature
    2. Digestion — Juvenile literature
    I. Title   II. Steele, Philip   III. Series
    612'.3   QP145

ISBN 0–333–45963–6

Photographic credits

t = top b = bottom l = left r = right

cover: Trevor Hill

4 The Hutchison Library; 5 S. & R. Greenhill; 6*t* Michael Holford; 6 The Ancient Art and Architecture Collection; 7 Vivien Fifield; 8 Vision International; 9*t* Tesco Stores Ltd; 9*b* Trevor Hill; 10*t* S. & R. Greenhill; 10*b* ZEFA; 12 Vision International; 13*t* Biophoto Associates; 13*b* Frank Lane Picture Agency; 14*t* Bruce Coleman Limited; 14*b* Vision International; 16*t* S. & R. Greenhill; 16*b* Vision International; 21*t*, 21*b* Science Photo Library; 22 Sporting Pictures; 25*t* Science Photo Library; 25*b* Vision International; 26 Sporting Pictures; 28 Trevor Hill; 29 S. & R. Greenhill; 30 Vivien Fifield; 31*t* Biophoto Associates; 31*b* Vision International; 32*t* The Hutchison Library; 32*b* Colorific; 33 Oxfam; 34 RHM Centre; 35*t* Vision International; 35*b* S. & R. Greenhill; 36 Vision International; 37*t* S. & R. Greenhill; 37*b* Camilla Jessel; 38 National Dairy Council; 39*t* Vision International; 39*b* Science Photo Library; 40 Biophoto Associates; 41 ZEFA; 42 Trevor Hill; 43*t* S. & R. Greenhill; 43*b* Vision International; 44 Science Photo Library; 45 Eric & David Hoskings

Note to the reader
In this book there are some words in the text which are printed in **bold** type. This shows that the word is listed in the glossary on page 46. The glossary gives a brief explanation of words which may be new to you.

Contents

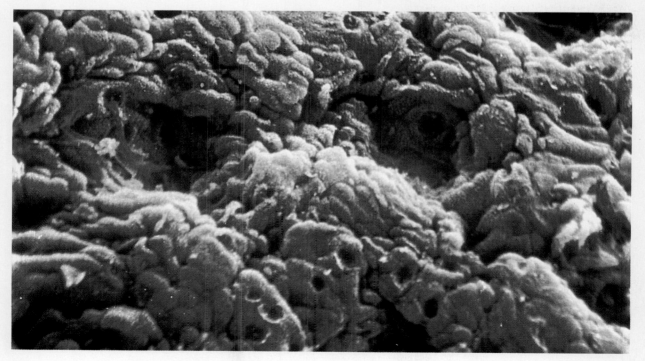

Introduction

If you had to make a list of your ten favourite things, you would probably put in something to eat or drink. We all enjoy the smell of fresh bread, the taste of an ice-cold drink on a hot day, or crunching into a crisp apple. Eating is something most of us enjoy. It is also vital to keep us alive.

Of course humans are not the only things that have to eat and drink. The meat and vegetables we eat for food were once living animals and plants themselves. Every living thing needs food.

Small animals, such as weasels or birds, catch and eat insects or smaller animals. In time it is the turn of these animals to become food for larger creatures. When the larger animals die their bodies break down and mix with the soil.

Plants make use of the substances that are broken down into soil to help them grow. Vegetables, grain and fruit are food for many different birds and animals, including humans. In this way the plant and animal worlds are linked together. Each depends on the other.

▼ A field of wheat is harvested in the late summer sunshine. All life on Earth depends on the Sun. The Sun's light and warmth makes plants grow. Animals eat the plants or they eat other animals which eat plants.

Who eats what?

A list of what animals feed on makes a complex pattern. For example, parts of a plant might be eaten by a mouse, a rabbit and an insect. The insect might be eaten by a lizard and the mouse could be eaten by a snake. A bird of prey might eat the insect, the rabbit, the mouse, the lizard and the snake. This pattern is called a **food web**.

Within a food web, there are several **food chains**. A food chain is one path in the web. For example, tiny plants in a rock pool are eaten by a sea snail. The snail might be eaten by a crab. The crab might be eaten by a squid which in turn is eaten by a fish.

Plants are usually at the bottom of a food chain. They are food for a great number of animals. Humans are usually at the top of a food chain. Very few other animals get the chance to eat us.

The food we eat

Food supplies the body with energy or the power to do things. In this book we shall learn about substances in the food which provide that energy. They are called **nutrients**. We shall find out about the way in which the body takes in food and makes use of it through **digestion**. It is important that we understand about food and digestion, for a healthy life depends upon healthy eating.

▲ This is a food network. Tiny plants and creatures that drift in the sea are eaten by larger creatures and small fish. These fish are eaten in turn by larger fish. These larger fish may be caught by seabirds or by humans.

► A family sits down to a meal in China. They are eating noodles, bean sprouts, seafood and fruit. Human beings eat both plants and animals. People in different parts of the world like to cook their food in different ways.

Hunters and farmers

Humans are the only animals that can grow their own food. All other creatures have to gather it or hunt for it. They may search out seeds, nuts and berries. They may catch other animals.

It was like this for the first people on Earth. They gathered parts of the plants that they found growing or they trapped wild animals. Every day a lot of time was taken up just finding enough food to stay alive. Early people moved from place to place. When all the food in one area was used up, they moved on. People still live in this way in some parts of the world.

▼ The first farmers lived in the river valleys of the Middle East and North Africa. This ancient Egyptian painting shows scenes from a harvest. Each year the River Nile flooded the desert. The floods left behind a layer of mud. Crops could be grown in this rich mud.

▼ Thousands of years ago, people had to hunt wild animals for their food. They painted pictures of themselves hunting and of their prey.

Crops and animals

Later, people learned how to save some of the seeds they had picked for food. They sowed them each year and waited for the plants to grow. They could be sure of having food later in the year. This meant that they could settle down and live in one place. They caught and tamed wild animals. Keeping these animals meant there was always a supply of milk and meat or skins and wool for making clothes.

A hard life

A bad winter or a dry summer meant that crops did not grow properly. The farmers had to grow enough food to last them through the times when they could not grow anything.

It was difficult to make the food last. The people found that meat, fruit and vegetables could be dried in order to stop them going bad. Salt could also be used to **preserve** food for the long winter months. Food could also be pickled in a liquid such as vinegar.

New machines

For hundreds of years, even people who were not farmers grew some vegetables and kept a few animals for food. Then, people started to live in big cities. There was no space there to grow food. Farmers had to grow more food to feed the people who lived in the cities. Farmers soon learned better ways of growing crops and looking after them. Machines were invented to do the farm work more quickly. New roads and railways were built to take the crops to markets in the cities. Ships were built to carry food and goods from one country to another.

In many countries today, only a few people grow crops or keep animals for their own food. Most people go to a shop to buy food that has been produced to sell.

▼ In the 1700s and 1800s many new machines, like this mechanical corn reaper, were invented. Farmers could now grow more crops and harvest them more quickly. Food was sent to be sold in the ever growing cities.

Food today

One hundred years ago there were only 1625 million people in the world. Today there are nearly 5000 million. Many people die because they do not have enough to eat. Many more go hungry. Enough food is grown in the world to feed everyone. The main problem is that crops are not always grown in the places where they are most needed.

How do farmers try to keep up with the more people asking for more food? Twenty years ago, a hectare field of wheat gave 1.4 tonnes of grain. Today it gives twice as much. This is partly because farmers use **fertilizers** to make the soil richer. Fertilizers contain the **chemicals** which plants need to grow well.

Farmers also use poisons called **pesticides**. These kill insects which might eat the crops we need for food. Farmers have also been helped by the large farm machines which have been invented. The machines mean that fewer people are needed to grow and harvest more crops.

◄ Today machines are often used to harvest fruit and vegetables. This machine is being used to help with the pineapple harvest in Hawaii. As the field workers pick the fruit, they place it on the conveyor belt.

Keeping food fresh

Once a crop has been harvested, it does not stay fresh for long. It soon starts to go bad. This is because it is being broken down by tiny creatures called **bacteria**. Some bacteria are harmless but others can make people ill if they eat them. There are many ways of keeping food fresh so that it lasts longer.

We still use old methods such as drying, salting, or pickling food. All these methods stop the bacteria destroying the food. Food also keeps better if it is kept cold. **Refrigeration** slows down the rate at which bacteria can work. Another way of preserving food is by **irradiation**. Rays are passed through food in order to kill the bacteria. Irradiation is a fairly new method. Tests are being done now to find if this way of keeping food fresh is safe.

▲ Supermarkets offer a wide range of produce. Food on the shelves has come from all over the world. It is sorted and neatly packaged.

The food we buy

A hundred years ago, most people ate fresh meat, fish and vegetables. They bought the food and prepared it themselves.

Today many people eat food that has been treated in some way or **processed**. Once the crops have been harvested or the animals killed, they are taken to factories. There, the food is cleaned and sorted. Then it may be chopped, mashed, frozen, dried or put in airtight cans. It is often cooked and made into food that is ready to eat, such as pies, biscuits or breakfast cereals. After the food has been put into packets or canned, it is sent to shops ready for us to buy.

◄ Bacteria cannot break food down quickly in cold conditions. Home fridges and freezers make it possible for us to keep food fresh for long periods.

Food and the body

Cars need petrol to make them go. A fire needs wood or coal before it can burn. Petrol, wood and coal are all kinds of fuel. The fuel that makes your body work is the food you eat. You use it up as you work, play, sleep and grow.

Your body is made up of billions of tiny parts called **cells**. Every single cell needs food to stay alive.

The food processor

Food enters your body at one end when you eat it. Unused parts of the food pass out at the other end when you go to the lavatory. In between, there is a long tube called the **digestive tract**. The food passes down this tube. The food that we eat cannot be used straight away by the body. As it passes through the digestive tract, the food has to be mixed, mashed and broken up. Only then can the nutrients in the food be used by the body.

▼ The body is a wonderful machine. It breaks down the food we eat and takes out the goodness we need to live.

▲ Playing can use up a lot of energy! Food is the fuel which keeps us going.

Digestion starts as soon as you take a bite of some food. Your teeth crunch the food into small pieces. The liquid in your mouth, called **saliva**, mixes with the food. Once the food has been swallowed, it passes down to the bag-like part we call the **stomach**. Here, more liquids mix with the food. It is broken up into even smaller pieces.

The next part of the digestive tract is called the **small intestine**. By now the food has been squeezed and churned into its smallest pieces. Nutrients pass out through the walls of the intestine into the blood which carries them around the body. The nutrients are stored in the **liver**.

Food waste, which the body cannot use, is left behind. It passes into the next section of the digestive tract, the **large intestine**. Here, water is taken from the waste and it becomes solid. The waste is finally pushed out of the body.

When you drink a liquid, your body takes in the water it needs to stay alive. Water is also squeezed into your blood from the food you have eaten. The amount of water in your blood is controlled by two filters called **kidneys**. Waste water is then passed from the body. It is called **urine**.

The digestive system

Mouth: Teeth chew up food. Saliva makes it slippery and starts to break it down

Oesophagus: The tube that carries food from the mouth to the stomach

Liver: A nutrient store and chemical factory

Stomach: Juices mix with the food. They contain further chemicals to break it down

Kidneys: Clean liquid waste and pass it out of the body

Small intestine: Nutrients pass through the wall of this tube into the blood

Large intestine: Last stages of digestion. Water is squeezed from the waste

Rectum: The end of the large intestine, through which waste is passed from the body

What is food made of?

▼ Bread fuels the body with carbohydrates. They give us the warmth and energy we need. Carbohydrates in bread, cereals, rice and potatoes take the form of starch.

All substances are made up of tiny parts called **molecules**. The food we eat is made up of quite large molecules. The process of digestion tears these molecules apart. The food is turned into simple nutrients made up of smaller molecules. These small molecules can be carried easily in the blood and can be used by the body's cells.

The energy givers

Most kinds of food contain many different nutrients. Some nutrients are known as **carbohydrates**. They provide much of the body's fuel. Carbohydrates are often found in the kinds of food we find filling, such as bread, rice, pasta and potatoes. This type of carbohydrate is called **starch. Sugar** is another type of carbohydrate. The foods which supply us with sugar have very few other nutrients.

Inside the body, starch and sugar, which are very complex, are broken down to form a very simple type of sugar called **glucose**. Glucose is a fuel needed by every cell in the body. Glucose joins up with the gas called **oxygen**, which passes from the air we breathe into the blood.

Together, glucose and oxygen release energy to power every process in your body.

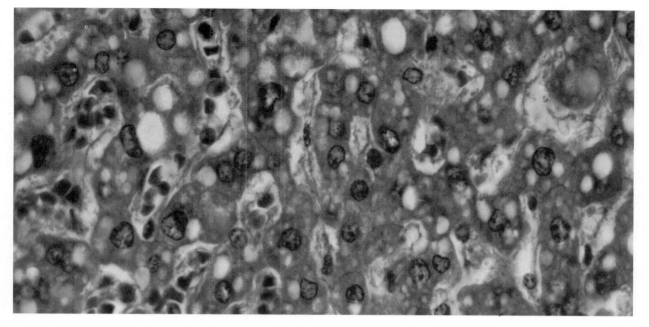

▲ The fats we eat quickly pass into the bloodstream. They give us energy. Here you can see droplets of fat collecting in the liver.

▼ The crew of a trawler raise their catch. Fish gives us plenty of protein. Protein helps the body grow, and also gives us energy.

Fats are also energy givers. Like carbohydrates, they are broken down inside the body and used as fuel. Small amounts of fat are also needed for body growth. Any extra fat may be stored as a layer of fat on your body. Eating too much fat is bad for your health.

Fats are found in red meat, lard, margarine and oil, and in dairy food such as milk, butter, cheese and yoghurt. Cakes, sweets and biscuits also contain fats.

The body builders

Proteins are another type of nutrient. They contain a chemical called **nitrogen**. Nitrogen is needed to build new cells and to repair old ones. Children need to eat plenty of protein because their bodies are still growing. Protein is found in meat, fish, cheese and eggs.

Our bodies cannot store extra protein for future use. Any protein that is not needed is passed out of the body in our urine.

Food at work

Food contains other substances that we need in order to stay healthy. **Dietary fibre**, or roughage, comes from green, leafy vegetables, the skins of fruit and other vegetables, and the husks of grain. It is not digested in the body and it does not pass through the walls of the intestine. Even so, it plays its part in keeping us healthy. Fibre gives bulk to the food which passes down the digestive tract. This bulk helps the intestine push the food along. Fibre exercises the intestine and keeps it strong.

▲ Leafy vegetables give us dietary fibre. This helps to move food through our intestines. Vegetables, like spinach, also give us vitamins and minerals, such as calcium and iron.

▼ The sun can make your body produce vitamin D when it shines on your skin. Vitamin D is also found in the fats and oils that we eat.

Releasing energy

There are many kinds of chemical found in the food we eat. Some of them are not turned into energy directly. They help the body in other ways. Some of these are known as **minerals**. A mineral called **calcium** is found in milk. It helps strengthen our teeth and bones. **Iron** is another mineral found in foods. It helps the blood carry oxygen.

Some of the other chemicals are called **vitamins**. Vitamins help release the energy from carbohydrates, fats and proteins.

There are several vitamins and each does a different job. Vitamin K, for example, helps blood clot so that it does not keep flowing from a wound.

Vitamins and minerals do not have to be broken down by digestion. They are carried in the blood to the liver. Most vitamins are stored in the liver until they are needed.

▼ This chart shows the full range of vitamins and some of the foods in which they are found. It also shows which parts of the human body are helped by which vitamins.

Vitamin	... found in	good for ...
A	dairy products vegetables fruit	 skin, ears, nose, throat, eyes
B$_1$ thiamine	cereals bread dried beans	 digestion, carbohydrate control
B$_2$ riboflavin	poultry dairy products meat	 skin, oxygen for cells
Niacin	meat fish dried beans bread, cereals	 nervous and digestive system
Vitamin C	citrus fruit green vegetables tomatoes	 teeth and gums, action of minerals
Vitamin D	milk dairy products fish cod-liver oil	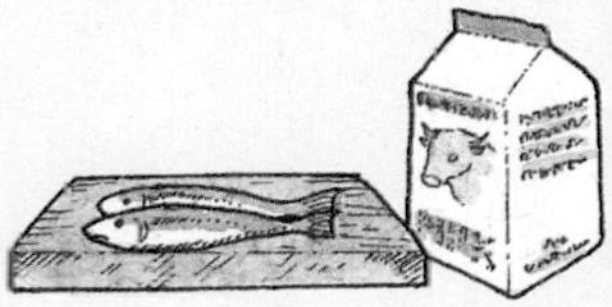 bones and teeth, controls calcium and phosphorus
Vitamin E	vegetable oil grains meat, especially liver	 cell tissues
Vitamin K	vegetables grains	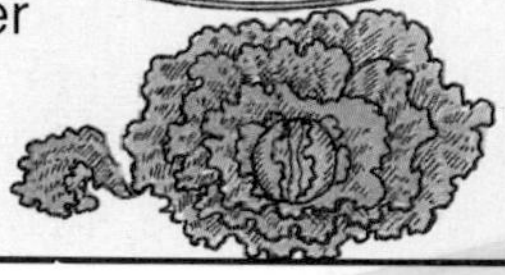 blood clotting

Biting and chewing

Our bodies get ready to digest food before we even take a bite. The smell and sight of food makes saliva squirt into our mouths. The saliva is a chemical produced by three pairs of **salivary glands**. These glands lie at the back of your mouth and under your tongue. They make over a litre of saliva every day.

Saliva is the first of many liquids that mix with the food on its way through the digestive tract. These juices contain chemicals called **enzymes**. Enzymes work on the food, breaking it down into simple parts. The enzyme in saliva acts on starch. Saliva also softens food so that it can be swallowed more easily.

▲ When you bite into a sandwich you use your incisors. Your other teeth then grind up the bread so that it can be swallowed.

◄ Scraps of food leave bacteria on your teeth. The bacteria make an acid which can eat into the tooth's outer covering of enamel. This makes the tooth decay and can be very painful. You should brush your teeth carefully after each meal, to keep them clean and healthy.

Breaking up the pieces

Teeth break up large pieces of food. They make them small enough to be swallowed. Humans can eat a wider variety of foods than almost any other animal. We can do this because our teeth have different shapes.

The sharp, square teeth at the front are called **incisors**. They are used for cutting, chopping and biting. At the sides are pointed teeth called **canines**. They are used for tearing food. The teeth at the back are big and flat. These **molars** have top surfaces that are wide and ridged. They grind the food into a smooth mixture. Once the food is well chewed and mixed with saliva, the tongue rolls it into a ball. The ball of food is pushed to the back of the mouth. It is ready to be swallowed.

All the teeth are rooted firmly in the two powerful **jaws**. The movements of these bones allows us to use our teeth. Each tooth is protected by a hard, white covering. Beneath this is a bone-like substance. The centre of each tooth is made up of a soft pulp.

Humans have two sets of teeth. The first set start to come through when a baby is about six months old. They are called the milk teeth. There are 24 milk teeth. At the age of five or six, the milk teeth begin to fall out. A new set of 32 adult teeth begin to grow.

▼ Digestion starts in the mouth. Our teeth prepare the food for swallowing. They must be very strong to keep chewing day after day, year after year. Here you can see the position of the teeth in the jaw and what a tooth looks like inside.

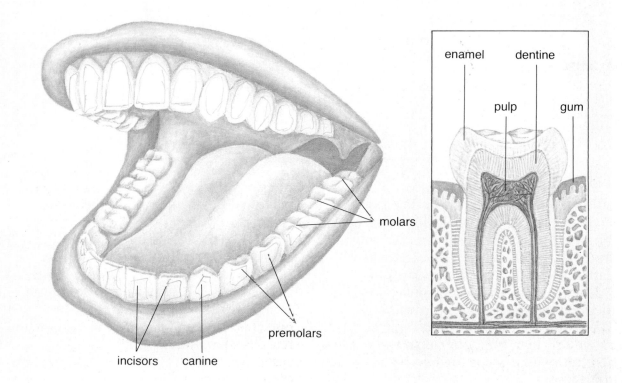

enamel   dentine   pulp   gum

molars

premolars

incisors   canine

Swallowing food

▼ Your mouth is used for breathing as well as for eating. A system of trapdoors makes sure that the air passages do not become blocked with food when you swallow.

Breathing   Swallowing

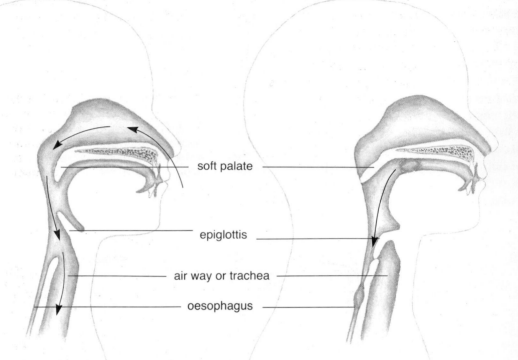

soft palate

epiglottis

air way or trachea

oesophagus

From the back of your throat, a tube called the **oesophagus** leads down into the stomach. At the top, the oesophagus opens up into the back of your nose. When you swallow, this opening is blocked off by a flap of skin called the soft palate.

Lower down, the oesophagus opens into the tube that takes air into your body. When you swallow this opening is also closed off, by a trapdoor called the **epiglottis**. This stops food going down into your lungs.

If food does enter the wrong tube, it makes you choke. Choking pushes air out of your body very fast. This blast of air pushes the food back to the top of the oesophagus or to the mouth.

Food does not simply drop down the oesophagus. Waves of movement squeeze it along. The movements are made by **muscles**. The muscles start to tighten and relax as soon as food enters the oesophagus. That is why you can swallow even if you are standing on your head.

Into the stomach

At the end of the oesophagus is a strong ring of muscle called a **sphincter**. This stops food which has passed from the oesophagus to the stomach being squeezed back. Your stomach is higher up in your body than you might expect. The picture below shows just where it is.

The wall of the stomach is muscular and stretchy. At its smallest, the stomach can hold about 0.5 litres. After a big meal it can hold as much as 2 litres.

Once food has reached the stomach, the process of breaking it up really gets going. Liquids called **gastric juices** pour into the stomach. They are made by glands in the stomach wall. The gastric juices contain more enzymes that work on the food. They also contain a chemical called **hydrochloric acid**. This acid is so strong that it could eat into the stomach itself as well as the food. The walls of the stomach are protected from the acid by a jelly-like lining called **mucus**.

During and after a meal, the stomach gives a squeeze about every 20 seconds. This churns up the food and allows the gastric juices to reach all of it. A small amount of the nutrients in the food passes through the stomach wall into the bloodstream. However, most of the food passes into the small intestine.

▼ Food is squeezed through the oesophagus into the stomach. If you could see inside your body, you would find that the outside of your stomach is smooth. The stomach wall is strengthened by powerful muscles. Inside, the stomach wall is lined with mucus.

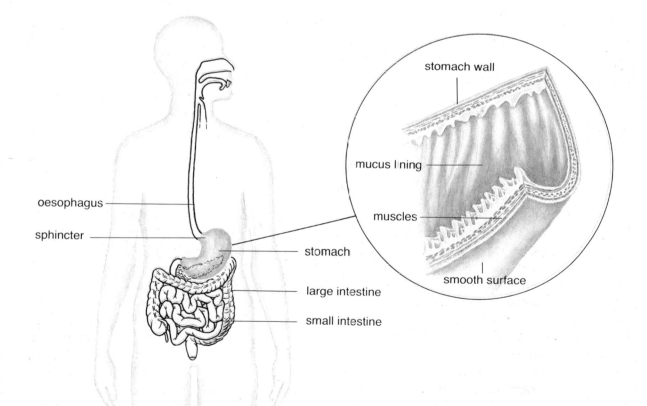

oesophagus

sphincter

stomach

large intestine

small intestine

stomach wall

mucus lining

muscles

smooth surface

Into the blood

Most food in the stomach is ready to move on after an hour or two. This is why you begin to feel hungry after a few hours. There is another sphincter between the lower part of the stomach and the small intestine. It is usually closed. From time to time the sphincter relaxes. When it does, a little half-digested food passes through it to the small intestine.

The small intestine

The whole digestive tract is about ten metres long. The small intestine alone is about seven metres. The first part of the small intestine is called the **duodenum**. Here, more juices attack the food. They contain a rich mixture of enzymes made in a part of the body called the **pancreas**. Other chemicals are added to the mixture from the **gall bladder**. It pours out a green liquid called **bile**. Bile acts on droplets of fat. It works like washing-up liquid by breaking up large droplets of fat into many tiny ones. This helps the enzymes reach the fat and break it down.

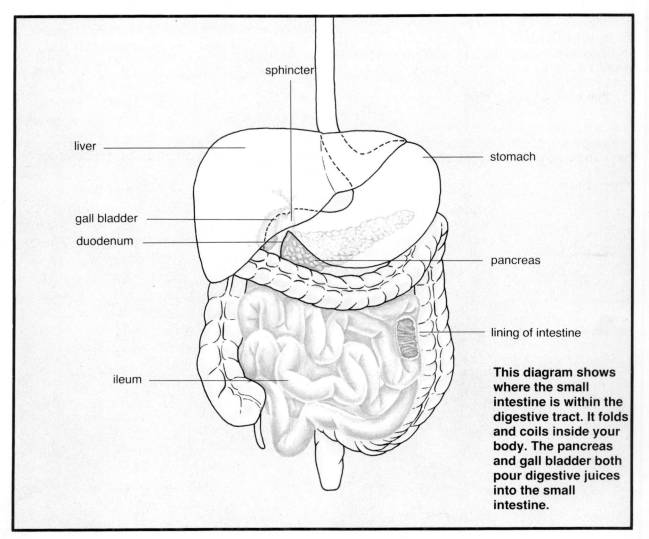

sphincter

liver

stomach

gall bladder

duodenum

pancreas

lining of intestine

ileum

This diagram shows where the small intestine is within the digestive tract. It folds and coils inside your body. The pancreas and gall bladder both pour digestive juices into the small intestine.

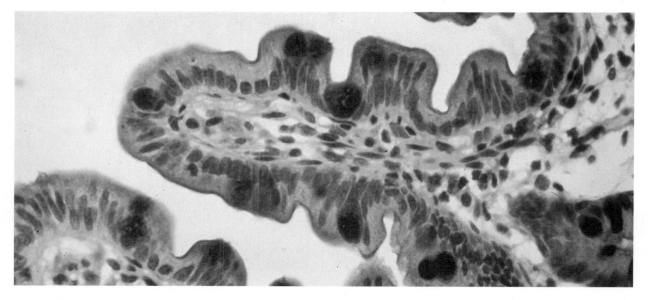

▲ Millions of villi stick out into the small intestine like tiny fingers. Almost all the nutrients that have been digested are taken into the villi. As well as blood vessels, each villus contains tiny tubes which take in some of the fats that have been digested.

▼ This is a microscope picture of green bile breaking fat down into smaller droplets, so that they can be absorbed into the body.

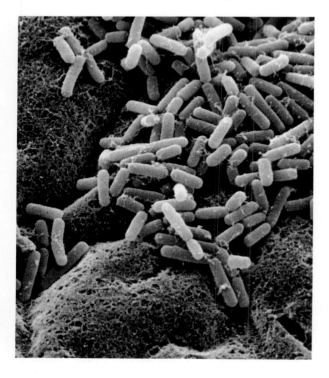

Passing on the nutrients

The food passes from the duodenum to a part of the small intestine called the **ileum**. Digestion is almost complete. No matter what you have eaten, it is broken up into the same basic parts. These parts are small and simple enough for the body to use them as fuel or as the building blocks for new cells.

Nutrients from the digested food now pass through the wall of the small intestine. The inside of this intestine is covered with millions of tiny, finger-like bumps. These are called **villi**. Each villus waves about in the food mixture. There are so many villi that if they were spread out they would cover a tennis court! This means that there is a huge surface through which nutrients can pass into the blood.

Next to the intestine there are masses of tiny tubes called **capillaries**. They carry blood around the body. The walls of the capillaries are only one cell thick. Nutrients from the intestine can squeeze through the tiny spaces between the cells and pass into the blood. Blood is the body's tranport system. It carries away the nutrients from the intestine to wherever they are needed.

The liver

Blood vessels are tubes which carry blood. The tiny blood vessels which lead from the small intestine join up to form larger and larger ones. They all join together to make a blood vessel called the **portal vein**. This leads to the liver. The blood flows along the portal vein carrying most of the nutrients from the digested food to the liver.

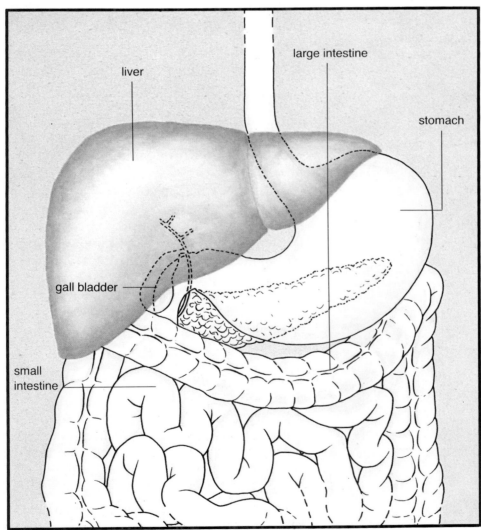

liver

large intestine

stomach

gall bladder

small intestine

▲ Some glycogen is stored in our muscles. When we call on our muscles to do some hard work, like these atheletes, the glycogen is quickly turned into glucose. The glucose is used as a fuel to release the energy we need. More reserves of fuel can be called up from the liver. Glycogen in the liver is also turned into glucose.

◄ The liver of an adult weighs about 1.5 kg. It is found next to the stomach. It sorts out the digested nutrients which enter the blood. Some are sent off to be used by the body. Others are sent for storage in the body. The liver can hold enough glycogen to keep the body going for about six hours.

Central store

The liver has many jobs to do. It acts as a store for nutrients. It sends them out to the parts of the body that need them.

Most of the carbohydrates you eat are broken down into glucose. Your body needs a steady supply of glucose to keep it going. However we do not have to keep eating carbohydrates all the time. Glucose can be stored in the liver as a substance called **glycogen**. Between meals, the liver is busy turning glycogen back into glucose for instant use. Glucose is carried in the bloodstream to every cell in the body.

Some of the fats we eat are needed for building new cells. The liver sends out any extra fat into the blood. In the long term it is stored as body fat. However, it can be changed back into body fuel when the body runs out of carbohydrates.

Protein from the food we eat is broken down into **amino acids**. The body cannot store amino acids. Instead, the liver takes out the amount needed for the moment. Any extra amount passes to the kidneys. It becomes **urea**. Urea is passed from our bodies in our liquid waste which is called urine.

Bile is made in the liver. It is piped from the liver to the gall bladder. It is stored there until it is needed to digest fats in the duodenum. Vitamins and iron are stored in the liver. Old blood cells go to the liver to be broken up and got rid of.

Central heating

A great many chemical processes are going on in the liver all the time. These processes give off heat. The liver is like a central heating boiler, keeping the body warm. Heat from this boiler is carried around the body in the blood vessels which act as the body's central heating pipes. This is how our bodies are able to stay at the same temperature whether it is hot and sunny or snowing outside.

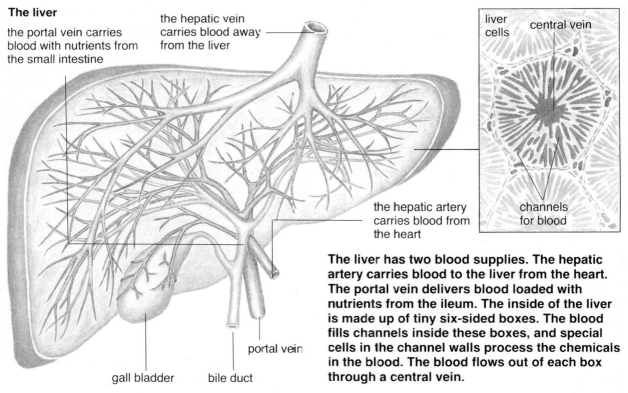

The liver

the portal vein carries blood with nutrients from the small intestine

the hepatic vein carries blood away from the liver

liver cells

central vein

the hepatic artery carries blood from the heart

channels for blood

gall bladder

bile duct

portal vein

The liver has two blood supplies. The hepatic artery carries blood to the liver from the heart. The portal vein delivers blood loaded with nutrients from the ileum. The inside of the liver is made up of tiny six-sided boxes. The blood fills channels inside these boxes, and special cells in the channel walls process the chemicals in the blood. The blood flows out of each box through a central vein.

23

The large intestine

▼ The large intestine, or colon, is much wider than the long, twisting small intestine. A meal may pass through the small intestine in five or six hours, but it may stay in the large intestine for a day or more.

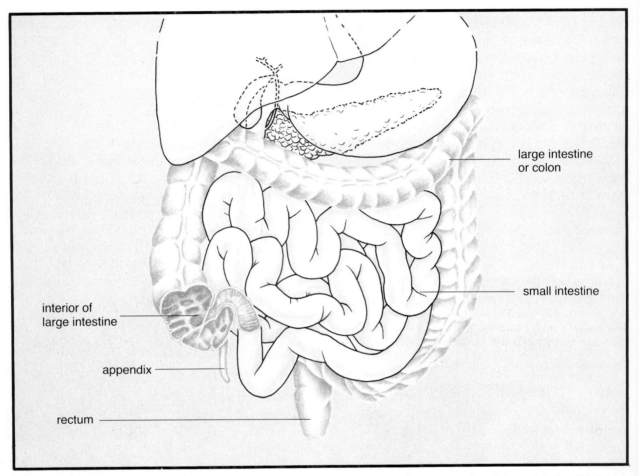

large intestine or colon

small intestine

interior of large intestine

appendix

rectum

Back in the digestive tract, the remains of food are being passed from the ileum to the large intestine or **colon**. It is called the large intestine because it is wider than the small intestine. It is only 1.5 metres long, so it is much shorter than the small intestine. It bends round in a U-shape.

The remains of the food enter the large intestine a little at a time. By the time food reaches the large intestine most of the digested nutrients have passed into the blood. All that is left is waste, which is mostly made up of dietary fibre. There is also a lot of water mixed in with it. This water is now taken out of the waste through the walls of the large intestine.

The waste now reaches the end of the large intestine, which is called the **rectum**. By now the waste is quite dry and solid. It passes out of your body when you go to the lavatory.

If plenty of fibre is eaten the waste is bulky and travels quickly through the large intestine. If too little fibre is eaten the waste travels more slowly. This can cause health problems.

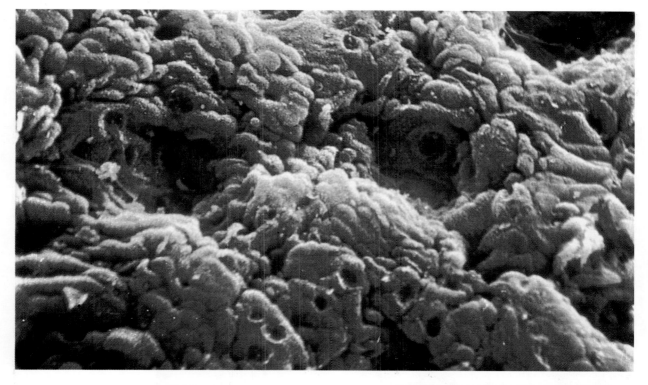

▲ The wall of the large intestine has strong muscles. Waves of movement push the bulky waste along to the rectum. Water squeezed from the waste can be passed back into the blood through the wall of the large intestine.

Now wash your hands

The large intestine is home to a large number of bacteria. Most of them are harmless to us. Some are helpful. They help to break down the food and some can help make useful vitamins which are taken into the body through the intestine wall. However some of the bacteria are very harmful. This means that it is important to wash your hands well after going to the lavatory. All traces of germs must be washed off.

By the time your breakfast has reached the large intestine, you are probably starting on lunch at the other end. The digestive process goes on smoothly, day and night. You do not have to think about it at all.

▲ Always wash your hands well after going to the lavatory. The germs of some diseases pass out of the body in waste matter. You could catch the disease and pass it on to someone else if you are not careful.

The kidneys

Humans can survive for several days without food. However we cannot do without water for more than two or three days. Water provides half of our total body weight. An adult's body contains about 20 litres of water. All the cells in the body contain water. There is water in the spaces between the cells, as well as in the blood and other body fluids.

Important substances such as salts and nutrients are carried in water. In fact, all the chemical changes that go on inside us happen in water.

Water is taken into our bodies and passed out again as we eat, drink, breathe, sweat and go to the lavatory. It is very important that the right amount of water is taken in and passed out. The water balance is checked by a kind of meter in the brain and in the digestive tract. If our bodies lose even one-tenth of their water and we do not replace it, we begin to feel very ill. This sometimes happens to people who are travelling in very hot countries.

◄ Our bodies are using up and loosing water all the time. If we lose just five per cent of our total water we feel thirsty. If we loose twenty per cent, we die. This happens in only two or three days of going without water. Water leaves our bodies as sweat or urine.

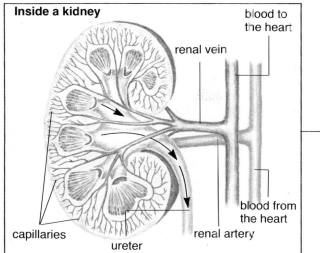

Inside a kidney

blood to the heart

renal vein

capillaries

ureter

blood from the heart

renal artery

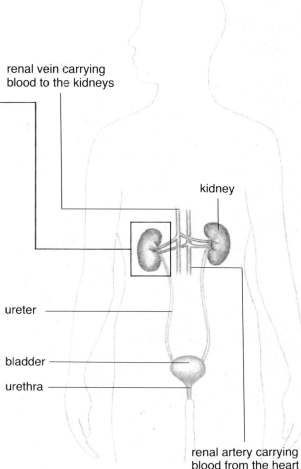

renal vein carrying blood to the kidneys

kidney

ureter

bladder

urethra

renal artery carrying blood from the heart

▲ Inside each kidney, there are millions of tiny blood vessels and many tiny tubes. Water and wastes from the blood are filtered as blood passes from the vessels into the tubes.

▶ Urine passes to the bladdder through the ureter. When the bladder is only a quarter full, our brain tells us that we need to go to the lavatory.

The cleaning system

One important way that water is removed from the body is in urine. Urine contains any extra water that the body does not need, together with wastes taken from the water in the blood. Urine is made in the kidneys. We have two kidneys. They are found close to the main blood vessels which run down the centre of our bodies. Blood passes through the kidneys. There it is filtered, as though it were passing through a fine sieve. Some of the water from the blood, together with unwanted chemicals and poisons, pass through the filter.

Precious chemicals and cells which the body needs are left behind. Most of the water with these chemicals and cells is then returned to the blood. A small amount of water containing the waste chemicals and poisons is left. This is the urine.

Waste water

The urine flows from each kidney through a tube called a **ureter**. The tubes lead to the bag-like **bladder**. As the bladder fills with urine we feel the need to go to the lavatory. The urine leaves the bladder through a tube called the **urethra**. Each day we pass out about a litre of urine. It may be slightly more or slightly less. This depends on how much we have had to drink, and whether we have lost water in other ways, such as by sweating.

All the blood passes through the kidneys to be cleaned almost 300 times in a single day. If one kidney stops working, the other one can still do the job on its own.

Input and output

Fuels provide energy. Energy gives machines the power to do things. Food is the fuel that provides your body with energy. Energy allows the body to work. Energy is measured in units called **calories**. Different kinds of food contain different amounts of calories.

How much food do we need?

A eleven-year-old girl uses up about 2200 calories of energy in a normal day. She has to eat food containing roughly the same number of calories if she is to keep her body fit and healthy.

If a girl eats food with more calories than she needs the extra food is stored as fat. She will put on weight. If she eats food with fewer calories then any stores of fat already there will be used up to supply her body with energy. She will get thinner.

We should know when to eat and when to stop. Part of the brain tells us when we are hungry or full. Most children balance the amount of food they eat each day with the amount of energy their bodies use up, without any problem.

However, people do not always eat only when they are hungry. Sometimes the sight, smell or taste of food tempts people to eat food they do not really need. Sometimes they eat just because it is time for a meal. If people eat more food than they need over a long period they often become fat.

Being much too fat or much too thin is very bad for your health. If people choose to eat only certain types or amounts of food, we say they are on a **diet**. People who are too fat often go on diets. Sometimes people diet too much. They eat so little that after a while they cannot eat a normal amount. They become very thin and ill. This is an illness called anorexia.

Input	calories	Output for one hour	calories
cup of tea, with milk and sugar	40	watching television	85
1 tsp sugar	25	reading	85
1 boiled egg	90	writing	115
cup of milk	100	cycling fast	600
2 rashers bacon	300	soccer	650
3 slices bread	240	tennis	450
100g chocolate	575	basketball	550
2 sausages	400	jogging	600
200g steak	390	hiking	400

▲ Here you can see the amount of calories provided by various kinds of foods. You can also see how many calories are used up by the body during one hour of exercise.

▶ The best way to keep weight down and stay fit is to take exercise. Hikers use their leg muscles. The muscles use up more energy than usual. They take it from the body's food input.

Burning it off

When a car travels fast, it uses up petrol more quickly than normal. The same is true of our bodies. Exercise, such as swimming or cycling, uses up calories more quickly than pastimes such as reading or watching television. The safest way to get rid of extra fat is to take more exercise rather than cutting down on the amount of food that you eat.

A poor diet

The word diet is also used to describe the whole range of food that someone eats. We say someone has a healthy diet or a poor diet. Sometimes people have plenty to eat, yet they still become ill.

This is because our bodies need a whole variety of nutrients to stay healthy. Missing out even tiny amounts of vitamins and minerals can cause serious diseases.

Becoming ill

Three hundred years ago the only way to travel from one continent to another was by a long sea voyage. It was very difficult to keep food fresh for months on end. The sailors used to live on hard biscuits and small amounts of salted meat. They often fell ill and even died from a disease called scurvy.

Then it was discovered that eating fresh lemons, oranges and limes stopped scurvy. Although they did not know it at the time, the sailors were suffering from a shortage of vitamin C. Eating citrus fruit supplied their bodies with this vitamin.

◄ Sailing ships of 300 years ago take on provisions on the North American coast. British sailors became known as limeys because they ate limes to prevent scurvy. Scurvy can be prevented by eating fresh fruit and vegetables which contain vitamin C.

In many countries today a lot of people suffer from **malnutrition**. This means that the food they eat does not contain the right variety of nutrients for good health. Malnutrition may happen even when there is plenty of food, if that food is all of the same kind. For example, there may be only rice or maize to eat. These do not provide all of the nutrients we need.

Children are growing so they are especially at risk from malnutrition. A lack of vitamin D can cause a disease called rickets. The child's bones become soft and do not grow properly. A lack of vitamin B may cause a disease called beriberi. A person with beriberi becomes very thin and has swollen legs and feet.

In many countries today most people have enough food to eat. The trouble is that people in these countries do not always realize that it is important to eat all kinds of different food. Always choosing the same food, or eating too much processed food, may cause bad health.

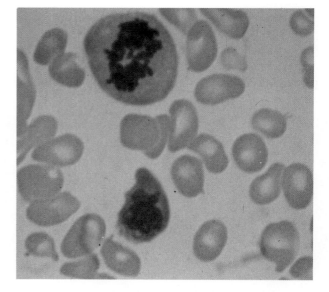

▲ There are two kinds of cells making up blood. White blood cells help the body fight disease. Red blood cells carry oxygen from the air we breathe around the body. To do this they need iron. If we do not take iron into our bodies, we may suffer from a disease called anaemia. Some of the blood cells shown here have been starved of oxygen in this way.

Extra vitamins

Fresh food contains the highest amount of vitamins and minerals. Vitamins can be lost if food is stored for a long time before it is eaten. They can also be lost if the food is overcooked.

Food manufacturers sometimes add extra vitamins to foods which do not have them. For example vitamin D is often added to milk. Some shops sell vitamin and mineral tablets to people who think they may not be getting enough in their food. However the best way to make sure you do get enough vitamins and minerals is to eat a good mixture of foods.

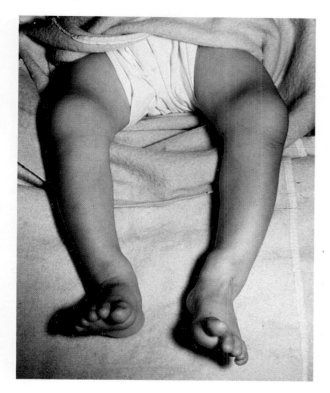

◀ Vitamin D can be found in fish oil, milk and egg yolk. A shortage of vitamin D can lead to a disease called rickets. Children with rickets have soft bones. Their legs may become mis-shapen. The best way of preventing the disease is to make sure that children are well fed.

Not enough food

▼ If the rains do not come to North Africa, the countryside turns into desert. Herds cannot graze and crops cannot grow. Many people may starve. They may have to rely on food sent from other countries.

The human body cannot survive long without food. Every day around the world, about 35 000 people die because they do not have enough food to eat.

At the same time, in other countries there is often more food than can be eaten. Whole 'mountains' of grain and 'lakes' of milk are put into storage. Thousands of tonnes of fruit and vegetables are thrown away or fed to animals.

Why do so many people in the world go hungry? In some places there is a shortage of water so that crops cannot grow. Sometimes the soil is washed away by sudden floods. If the people are starving they often do not have enough money to buy food supplies from outside the area. Sometimes governments get people to grow crops to make money rather than for food. Sometimes there are wars which stop people growing or harvesting their crops.

▲ So much wheat has been harvested in this farming town in Nebraska, USA, that the grain has been piled up on the main street. While some countries produce too much food, other countries have shortages.

▲ Welsh children join a sponsored walk to raise money to offer some help to people starving in other lands. Groups called charities collect the money. They can send emergency food supplies. They can set up long-term projects to help the farmers in these countries.

Helping out

When a lot of people are starving, food is often sent by those countries which have a lot, along with money and medical aid. There are many groups in these countries which collect money from people so that it can be used to help the starving people of the world.

Food supplies help in the short term. They may stop people starving during a **famine**. In the long term, however, the local people must be helped to produce food for themselves. A supply of clean water, tools for farming and seed may be more important than gifts of food. There are many groups which work with people to help them prevent food shortages. One of these groups is called Oxfam.

Helping in North Africa

Dogani Bere is in Mali, in North Africa. For several years there was little or no rainfall. The villagers of Dogani Bere went hungry. In 1984 a worker from Oxfam came to the area to see what could be done to help. Later, Oxfam helped the villagers to build two small dams. Oxfam raised money for the villagers to buy transport and cement. It gave the villagers some expert advice. The villagers worked very hard.

Today the dams are finished. They allow water to be stored so that it can be used the next time there is no rain.

The wrong kind of food

Having too much food brings its own problems. In some parts of the world, there is so much food that many of its useful parts are thrown away.

People like to cook with white flour. This is made by removing the outer husks of the wheat. People like to eat white rice which has also had its husks removed. The husks of these grains contain most of the nutrients. Brown flour and brown rice are better for us. They are **wholefoods**. Nothing has been taken away from the food or added to it.

In the past people did not realize that our bodies need the kind of fibre found in brown bread and rice. We have learned about the effect of fibre on the digestive tract. Too little fibre can make us very ill.

▼ Wheat is ground into flour in milling machines. Wholemeal flour, which includes the husk of the grain, is better for the digestive tract. It adds fibre to the food we eat.

► Meat fat is high in cholesterol. Small amounts are not harmful, but if we always eat too much it is bad for us.

▼ Oils made from sunflower seeds can lower our cholesterol level. Oils made from peanuts and olives do not affect the cholesterol level very much.

Unhealthy food

In countries where there is plenty of food, it is often processed. Sugar and fat may be added. Our bodies can make use of sugar as a carbohydrate. However, sugar gives the body no other useful nutrients. It does not contain a single mineral or vitamin. It contains no protein or useful fat. Eating sugar does our bodies little good. Too much sugar makes our teeth decay and makes us fat.

Our bodies need small amounts of certain kinds of fat. When we eat processed food, it is easy to eat more fat than we need. Pies, biscuits, cakes and crisps all contain lots of hidden fat.

Animal products such as meat, eggs and milk contain a fatty substance called **cholesterol**. We need small amounts of cholesterol but too much is bad for us. It builds up in the blood and clogs up the blood vessels around the heart. It causes heart disease.

In countries where people do not eat large amounts of meat or dairy produce, they do not suffer much from heart diseases. Vegetable fats contain less cholesterol. Cooking with vegetable oil and eating vegetable-based margarine is a good way of cutting down on cholesterol.

Eating for health

When a country becomes more developed, the way of life of the people who live there often changes. There are large cities where everyone seems to be in a hurry. The kind of food people eat changes, too. People buy food that is easy to prepare. It can be taken from a tin or a packet and eaten quickly.

These foods are called **convenience foods**. Fish fingers, sausages, oven-ready chips, instant snacks and puddings, sweet bars and crisps are all easy to eat. The trouble is that if we eat too many of these processed foods, we upset the proper balance of nutrients in our diet.

All kinds of food

A healthy diet contains a wide range of different foods. We call it a balanced diet. A balanced diet should include plenty of carbohydrate, especially starch, some protein and small amounts of fat.

Vitamins and fibre should be provided by plenty of fresh fruit and vegetables. There should not be too much sugar or salt added to the diet. We can get all the sugar and salt we need from food without adding anything to it.

◄ The food shown here is just as tasty as processed food and is much better for you. A balanced diet often includes wholefoods, which have none of their fibre taken away. The fresher the food, the more likely it is to contain plenty of vitamins.

▲ Sweets are all right as an occasional treat, but too many can be bad for you. The sugar causes bacteria to grow in your mouth. These bacteria attack your teeth. Eating sweets also means that you have less appetite for other foods.

▼ It is especially important that young people, old people and those who are ill eat a healthy diet. Nutritionists in hospital need to plan menus carefully.

Planning a diet

People who study diet and its effect on the body are called **nutritionists**. Ideas about diet have changed in recent years. People used to think that carbohydrates were bad for them and made them fat. Now nutritionists believe that it is all right to get most of your energy from complex carbohydrates like bread, potatoes or pasta. You need to keep down the intake of carbohydrates from fat and sugar.

School lunches

People's eating habits are made when they are very young. Once you are used to eating very sweet things and lots of fried food, it is not always easy to retrain your tastes.

In many places nutritionists are making sure that school meals include more wholefoods and fewer fatty foods. If people are to be healthy as adults, and if they want to stay healthy in old age, they must eat a healthy, balanced diet when they are young.

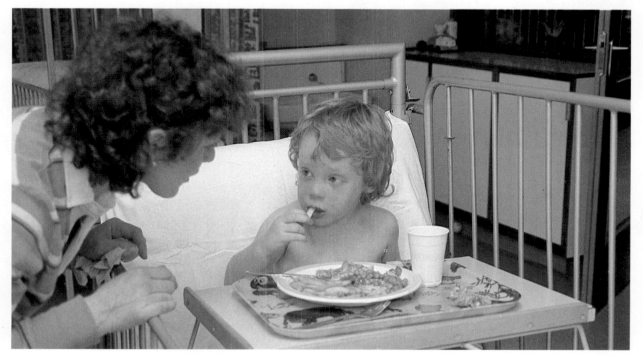

Food and illness

▼ Milk may carry the bacteria of several diseases. Most of the milk we drink is pasteurized. It has been heated in large machines like these to destroy the bacteria. Everything is kept very clean.

There are millions of bacteria all around us. They are in the air, on our bodies and in our food. Many bacteria are helpful. They are used in making cheese, yoghurt, wine and some medicines. Bacteria in our intestines even help us digest our food. However, some bacteria make us ill.

The bacteria have to enter our bodies in order to affect us. If we eat food which contains harmful bacteria we may become ill. Some bacteria make poisons as they grow. Others attack the digestive system when we swallow them. Both kinds of bacteria give people **food poisoning**. They may make people be sick. They give people **diarrhoea**.

Diarrhoea makes the body pass out its solid waste matter very often. The body also passes out too much water which makes the body dry, or dehydrated. These are both ways in which the body gets poison out of its system in a hurry.

Clean food

Bacteria grow best in moist, warm places. A nice, warm kitchen is ideal! Bacteria are easily spread from our bodies, from animals, from cuts and grazes. They can easily get on to our hands and so be passed on to our food. **Always wash your hands before touching food**.

When food is cooked well the bacteria are killed. Fresh food should be covered. Keep cooked food in the fridge.

▶ Many people poison their bodies with the things they choose to eat and drink. Alcohol in large amounts is a poison, and yet all over the world people drink too much of it. This damages the liver. This poster, from the Soviet Union, warns people of the dangers of alcohol.

▼ These bacteria are of a kind called salmonella. They are common in meat and poultry. They can cause sickness and diarrhoea if they are eaten. However, they are killed when food is well cooked.

ЗЛОУПОТРЕБЛЕНИЕ АЛКОГОЛЕМ

ТАК РАЗВИВАЮТСЯ

ГАСТРИТЫ, КОЛИТЫ, ЯЗВЕННАЯ БОЛЕЗНЬ, ЗАБОЛЕВАНИЯ ПЕЧЕНИ

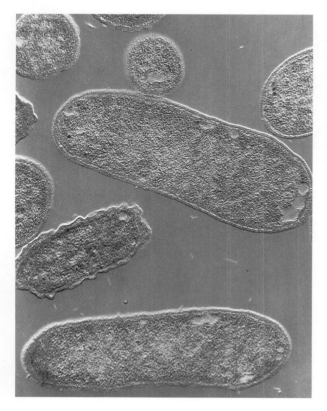

Passing on germs

Other kinds of bacteria can also pass from one person to another through food. If the cook has a cold and sneezes on the food, anyone eating that food is likely to get a cold. Some very serious diseases can be spread by food and through water supplies which contain harmful bacteria. Polio is a disease which can be spread in this way. It can damage people's muscles. Cholera is another disease which is very dangerous. It gives people such bad diarrhoea and sickness that they often die.

In many countries people are **immunized** against catching diseases such as these. They are injected with a small amount of the germ. The body makes substances which help it to fight against the disease. These substances stay in the blood so that the body is protected in the future. If we keep food and water clean we can help the fight against the spread of disease.

Medicine today

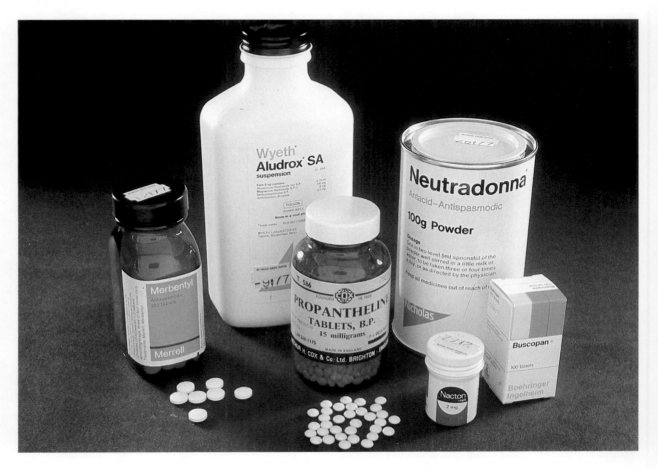

In 1928 a Scottish scientist called Alexander Fleming discovered a powerful new medicine. It was the first of a whole new range of drugs called **antibiotics**. Antibiotics are very useful as they kill bacteria without harming human cells.

Many illnesses of the stomach and intestines, such as gastroenteritis, get better by themselves in a day or two. Bad cases may need to be treated with antibiotics. Antibiotics, such as penicillin, kill the bacteria which are causing the illness.

In hospital

Surgeons can carry out many different operations on the digestive tract, just as they can on other parts of the body. For example, it is quite common for surgeons to remove an **appendix**. The appendix is a short tube which leads off the large intestine. The appendix is no longer useful to the human body. It sometimes becomes infected by food which has become stuck in it. This is painful and can be dangerous. The appendix has to be taken out. We can manage very well without it.

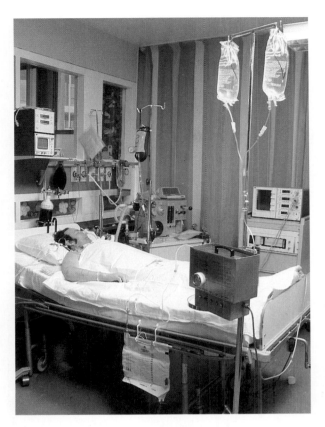

▲ This man is very ill in hospital. An intravenous drip passes nutrients through tubes straight into his bloodstream.

Providing nutrients

After some operations, or when people are very ill, they may not be able to digest food properly. The nutrients that they need can be fed straight into the patient's bloodstream through an **intravenous drip**. Intravenous means 'through a vein'. A drip bypasses the whole digestive system. A liquid containing glucose and salts flows down a tube, and through a needle into one of the patient's veins. The amount of liquid passing into the blood can be carefully controlled. Doctors take samples of blood and test it to make sure that it contains the correct level of glucose and salts.

Machines to the rescue

If the kidneys stop working properly dangerous wastes build up in the blood. A **kidney machine** can take over the job of cleaning the blood. A living kidney works all the time. It is small enough to fit into one hand. An artificial kidney is a large machine. The patient has to be attached to it for several hours twice a week. Kidney machines have saved countless lives.

A kidney machine

A kidney machine takes blood from the patient's body. It pumps the blood through a filter. When the blood has been cleaned, it is returned to the body.

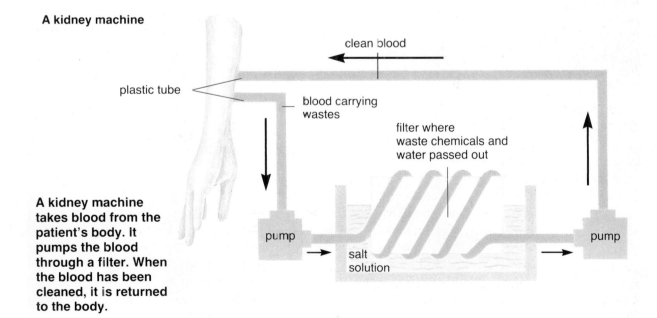

clean blood

plastic tube

blood carrying wastes

filter where waste chemicals and water passed out

pump

salt solution

pump

Public health

In many parts of the world, people live in crowded towns and cities. It is easy for bacteria to be spread in such places. They can spread in food and in waste. Preparing food and getting rid of waste has to be carefully controlled to prevent the spread of disease.

Getting to market

Inspectors check that food is stored properly before it reaches the shops. Meat and fish and dairy products must be kept cool or refrigerated. Grain, fruit and vegetables must be stored where they cannot be spoiled by insects, rats or mice.

Buying and selling

Inspectors make sure that only food of the right quality is put on sale. The next time you go shopping look carefully at the labels on the food. Most processed food must now be stamped with a date that shows when it must be sold by. This makes sure that the customer knows whether the food is fresh.

Labels also have details of what the food contains. Many processed foods have chemicals added to them. Some of the chemicals are put in to add flavour or colour to the food. Others may be added to preserve the food.

▼ Many diseases can be spread by preparing food in dirty places. People who work in kitchens have to keep themselves and everything they use very clean. This hotel food inspector is checking that the rules are being followed.

Scraps of food

Restaurants and hotels must also be inspected. Their kitchens must be kept clean. Food scraps and other rubbish must be removed daily.

Wherever people live it is important that food scraps and rubbish are collected regularly. They must be taken away to a dump and buried or burnt. Rotting food attracts flies and spreads disease.

Getting rid of waste

Public health also depends upon a healthy system of getting rid of human waste. This waste is called **sewage**. It is piped from lavatories to a central works. At the sewage works it is treated with chemicals and filtered to make it harmless. If sewage is not treated and got rid of carefully, terrible diseases can be spread very easily.

► When people are taught to cook, they must also learn how to handle food. Hands must be washed. Cookers, cutlery, dishes and pans must all be spotless. Bacteria thrive on dirt.

► Before sewage works were built, towns and cities were very unhealthy places. Waste was simply tipped into the streets. Today sewage is passed through underground pipes to places where it can be treated to make it safe.

Food in the future

Today there are 5000 million people living on Earth. By the year 2000 there will be 6100 million mouths to feed. How will enough food be produced for so many people?

Meat or vegetables?

Wherever we live in the world, we need a balanced diet. The problem is that most of the protein eaten in the richer countries comes from animals. Rearing animals is a very wasteful way of using the land. Much of the grass eaten is used to give the animal energy rather than just to make protein. It would be better if we could get protein from the plants growing on the land in a more direct way.

Plants such as soya beans are a good source of protein. Soya has been used for a long time in Asia. Now it is being used in other parts of the world. It is not a very tasty food but it can be given flavour. It can be made into a kind of cheese called bean curd or tofu. It can also be made into a substance rather like meat. Soya protein is already added to minced beef. It is a cheap way of making it go further. In future soya could be a cheap source of protein to make the world's food supplies go further.

▼ In space, there is no air and objects are weightless. However, in the future it might be possible to build huge spacecraft where crops could be grown and harvested by robots. Scientists have already tried to find out how plants grow on board a spacecraft. This experiment was carried out on the American space shuttle.

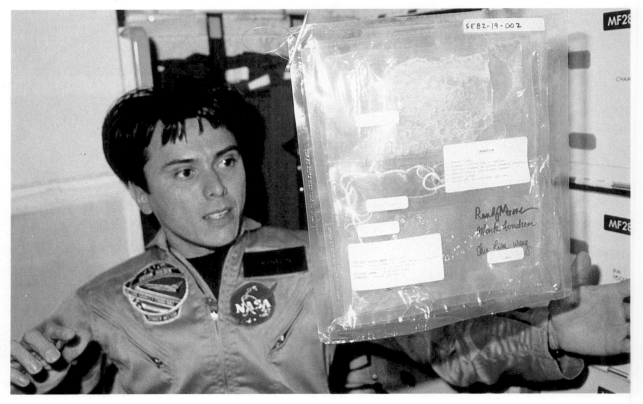

Harvest from the sea

Most of the food we eat comes from the land, yet the oceans cover two-thirds of the world's surface. Catching fish can be a matter of chance. Fish are one of the few creatures that we still have to hunt for food. Freshwater fish such as trout are reared in fish farms but we need to learn much more about farming sea fish. Perhaps one day there will be huge farms under the sea. Fish can be bred there and seaweeds harvested for food.

Food and science

In the future there will be new ways of preserving food, and new ways of processing food. Convenience foods will always be popular but more people will also realize that healthy food is best. New wonder foods may be dreamed up by scientists. All this will only be worthwhile if everyone on Earth has enough food to live a healthy life.

▲ Eilat is in Israel, on the edge of the desert. Irrigation makes it possible to grow crops there. Jets of water are sprayed over the fields.

▼ In the future, farms may be built deep beneath the waves. Fish and shellfish could be grown in large underwater tanks. Seaweed could be grown on the ocean floor and harvested.

Glossary

amino acids: the important substances the body gets by breaking down the proteins in food

antibiotics: drugs that can be given to kill bacteria in the body without harming body cells

appendix: a short tube leading from the large intestine. In animals it helps digest cellulose but serves no purpose in humans

bacteria: tiny creatures that can only be seen with a strong microscope. Many bacteria are helpful to us. Some cause diseases

bile: a bitter, greenish liquid made in the liver and stored in the gall bladder. Bile helps digest fat

bladder: the bag in which waste liquid collects before it passes out of the body

blood vessel: any tube which carries blood through our bodies

calcium: a substance in the food we eat which builds up our bones and teeth

calorie: a unit used for measuring the amount of energy each kind of food gives. It is also called a kilocalorie

canine: one of four sharp teeth, near the front of your mouth, which are used for tearing and cutting food

capillary: a very tiny tube which carries blood in and out of every part of the body, no matter how small

carbohydrate: a substance made by plants. Animals eat carbohydrate to give them energy

cell: a very small part or unit of a living animal or plant. Most living things are made up of millions of cells

chemicals: any substances which can change when joined or mixed with another substance

cholesterol: a fatty substance carried in the blood. Too much is bad for us and causes heart disease

colon: another name for the large intestine where water is passed into the body, leaving behind unwanted waste and fibre

convenience food: food which has been processed so that it needs little or no preparation before it is eaten

diarrhoea: a disorder of the intestine in which waste matter does not become solid

diet: the range and kind of foods a person eats

dietary fibre: the hard, woody parts in the fruit and vegetables we eat. It is not digested, but it gives bulk to our food as it passes through our bodies

digestion: the way foods are broken down into simpler forms which can be used in the body as fuel and to build new cells

digestive tract: the system of tubes which pass food through our body

duodenum: the part of the intestine that leads out of the stomach. In the duodenum juices mix with food helping to digest it

enzymes: substances made in the body which break food down into simpler parts

epiglottis: a trapdoor which prevents food blocking our breathing tubes when we swallow

famine: a time when there is little or no food in a country or region because of a disaster like a drought

fat: one of the basic substances which the body needs to stay healthy. Fat is a source of energy and is found in some plant and all animal foods

fertilizer: chemicals that are used to make crops grow more strongly

food chain: the sequence in which one animal eats another animal, and then that animal eats another creature, and so on

food poisoning: when a person is made ill by the food they have eaten

food web: a pattern which shows how different animals feed upon each other

gall bladder: a bag that lies near the small intestine. It acts as a store for bile

gastric juices: liquids which pour into the stomach to help break up food

glucose: a kind of simple sugar which the body uses as fuel to keep working

glycogen: the form in which glucose is stored in the blood

hydrochloric acid: a strong liquid found in the stomach. It helps us to digest food

ileum: the part of the small intestine where digested food is absorbed into the body

immunize: to give someone a dose of specially treated germs so that their body can build up substances which can fight those germs

incisor: one of the sharp teeth at the front of our mouths, used for cutting and chopping food

intravenous drip: a way of passing food and other chemicals directly into someone's bloodstream using a tube and a needle. It is used when someone is very ill or after a serious operation

iron: a metal mineral found in many foods. Our bodies need small amounts of iron to stay healthy

irradiation: a way of preseving food. Special rays are used to kill off any germs in the food

jaw: the bony part of the mouth which holds the teeth

kidney machine: a machine which cleans the blood when someone's kidneys do not work properly

kidneys: two small organs found on either side of your backbone, near your waist. The kidneys filter your blood, removing wastes and poisons

large intestine: part of the intestine at the end of the digestive tract where water is taken back into the body, leaving behind solid waste

liver: the body's chemical factory. In the liver, the chemical parts of the food are built up or broken down, so that your body is always supplied with the right food

malnutrition: when someone does not get enough goodness from food in order to stay healthy

minerals: chemicals such as iron and calcium, which the body needs in tiny amounts to stay healthy. Small amounts of the chemicals are found in many different foods

molar: one of the teeth at the back of the jaw, used for grinding food

molecule: the smallest unit of a substance, made up of at least two atoms

mucus: a jelly-like substance. Mucus coats the walls of the stomach and other organs. It makes the walls slippery and helps protect them

muscle: a type of material in the body which shortens in order to produce movement

nitrogen: a substance which the body needs to help build new cells

nutrients: the basic substances found in all foods which the body uses for fuel, and for growth and repair

nutritionist: a person who studies the different kinds of food we eat and the goodness they contain

oesophagus: the tube that leads from your throat down to your stomach

oxygen: a gas found in the air. We need it to breathe. It is used in our bodies to join up with food to release the energy we need to stay alive

pancreas: part of the body that lies below the stomach. It makes digestive juices which pour into the small intestine

pesticides: chemicals which are sprayed on to crops to kill insects which may spoil them

portal vein: a large blood vessel which carries blood containing digested food from the small intestine to the liver

preserve: to treat food to make it last longer without going bad

processed: describes food which has been treated, cooked or preserved

proteins: one of the basic substances found in food. Proteins are needed to build and repair the body. Meat, eggs, fish and some plants are rich in protein

rectum: the end part of the large intestine where solid waste is passed from the body

refrigeration: the use of a machine to keep foods at a low temperature

saliva: the liquid in your mouth. Saliva contains chemicals that start breaking up the food and make it easier to swallow

salivary gland: one of the places under your tongue and inside your cheeks where saliva is made

sewage: a mixture of water and waste which is carried away from buildings in underground pipes

small intestine: the first and longest part of the intestine. When food reaches the small intestine, it is finally broken down. The digested food is passed into the body through the wall of the intestine

sphincter: a circular bunch of muscle which seals the end of various tubes in the body

starch: a substance found in food such as bread and potatoes

stomach: a bag-like part of the body where food is broken up after being swallowed

sugar: a substance found in foods such as fruit, milk, sugar-cane and vegetable roots

urea: a chemical made in the liver out of protein that we do not need

ureter: a tube which carries waste from the kidneys to the bladder

urethra: a tube which carries waste water out of the body from the bladder

urine: the waste water that passes out of the body. It contains wastes cleaned out of the bloodstream

villi: one of the millions of tiny 'fingers' that stick out into the small intestine. Digested food is taken into the bloodstream through the villi

vitamins: one of a number of complicated chemicals which we need in tiny amounts to stay healthy

wholefood: food which has had nothing added to it and nothing taken away when we buy it

Index